yukibooks.com/b/

baby

bébé

boy

garçon

friends

amis

girl

fille

smile

sourire

cry

pleurer

hair

cheveux

eye

oeil

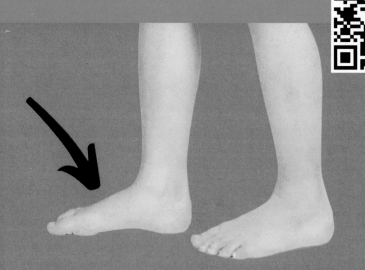

foot

pied

hand

main

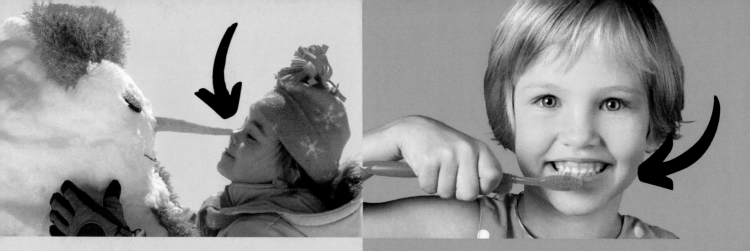

nose

nez

teeth

dents

ear

oreille

tongue

langue

sun

soleil

moon

lune

star

étoile

tree

arbre

bird

oiseau

coat

🇫🇷 **manteau**
🇨🇦 **froque**

pants

pantalon

dress

robe

shoes

chaussures

red

rouge

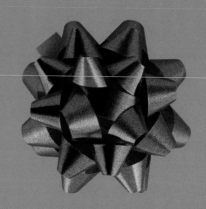

blue

bleu

yellow

jaune

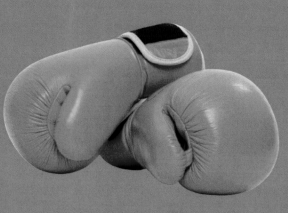

pink

rose

white

blanc

green

vert

black

noir

multicolored

multicolore

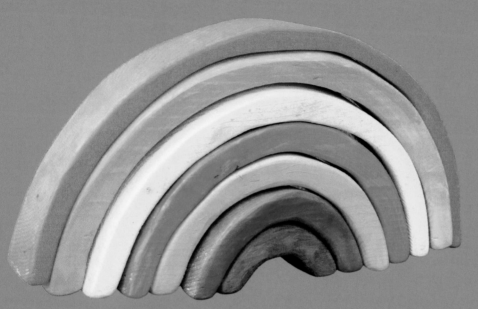

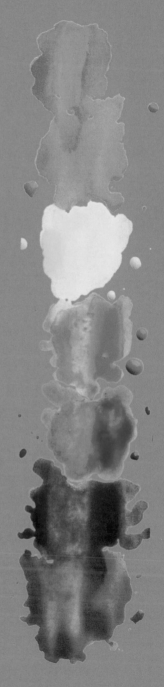

rainbow

arc en ciel

apple

pomme

banana

banane

tomato

tomate

orange

orange

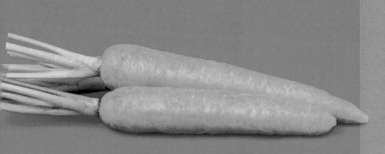

carrot

carotte

peas

petits pois

potato

pomme de terre

corn

🇫🇷 maïs

🇨🇦 blé d'inde

lemon

citron

grapes

raisins

pear

poire

watermelon

pastèque

zucchini

courgette

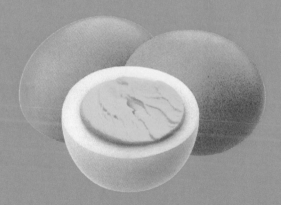

egg

oeuf

mushroom

champignon

square

carré

circle

rond

rectangle

rectangle

triangle

triangle

cat

chat

dog

chien

fish

poisson

cow

vache

duck

canard

chick

poussin

hen

poule

frog
grenouille

pig
cochon

rabbit
lapin

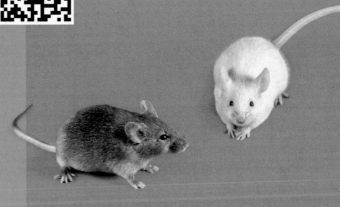

mouse
souris

horse

cheval

sheep

mouton

flower

fleur

butterfly

papillon

ladybug

coccinelle

snail

escargot

cake

gâteau

bread

pain

clock

horloge

key

clé

book

livre

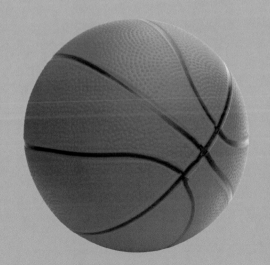

ball

ballon

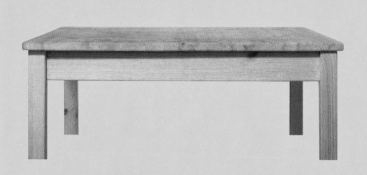

table

table

plate

assiette

chair

chaise

high chair

chaise haute

fork

fourchette

knife

couteau

spoon

cuillère

cup

tasse

baby bottle

biberon

glass

verre

bed

lit

crib

lit bébé

teddy bear

🇫🇷 ours en peluche

🇨🇦 toutou

pacifier

tétine

towel

serviette

sink

lavabo

toothbrush

brosse à dents

soap

savon

toilets

toilettes

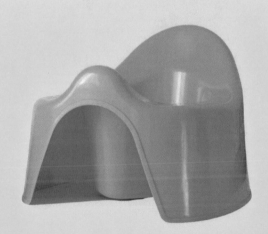

potty

pot

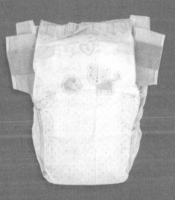

diaper

couche

car
🏴 voiture
🍁 char

bike
🏴 vélo
🍁 bicycle

plane
avion

boat
bateau

firetruck

camion de pompier

train

train

toys

jouets

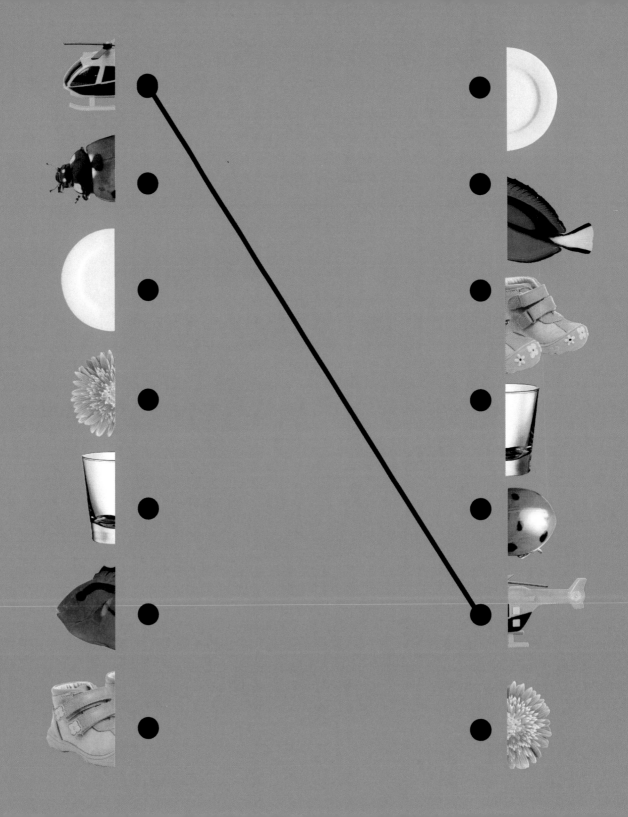

Made in United States
Orlando, FL
12 November 2023